Holy Howlers

Collected and Compiled

by

Patricia J. Hunt

MOORLEY'S Print & Publishing

© Copyright 1999

All rights reserved. No part of this publication may be
reproduced, stored in a retrieval system, or
transmitted, in any form or by any means,
electronic, mechanical, photocopying, recording
or otherwise, without the prior
written permission of the publishers.

British Library Cataloguing in Publication Data.
A catalogue record for this book is available
from the British Library.

ISBN 0 86071 539 6

MOORLEY'S Print & Publishing
23 Park Rd., Ilkeston, Derbys DE7 5DA
Tel/Fax: (0115) 932 0643

CONTENTS

PART I - CHILDREN　　　　　　　　　　　　　　　Page

a) General 5

b) Misheard 11

c) Christmas 12

d) Children's Prayers 13

e) Comments on the Clergy 14

f) The collection 16

g) Phonetic Spellings 17

h) Verbal Answers 17

i) Written Answers 20

j) Definitions 23

PART II - THE LIGHTER SIDE OF ADULT CHURCH LIFE

a) General 27

b) Mainly Clerical 32

c) Epitaphs 35

d) From Parish Magazines and Other Literature 36

Acknowledgements 38

PART I
With ... about ... for ... by CHILDREN

a) GENERAL

The mother of a Sunday School child, herself a Sunday School teacher, was about to go into hospital to have her fourth baby. The eldest boy, aged ten, was very disgruntled at the thought of losing his mother for a few days.
'I don't know why you have to go to hospital,' he declared, 'you've had three of us already. You ought to know how to do it yourself by now.'

☺ ☺ ☺ ☺ ☺

Stern father: I hear that you didn't go to Sunday School today, but that you went and played football instead.
Guileless boy: No I didn't, dad. I went fishing, and I've got a basket of fish here to prove it.

Knutsford Parish Church Magazine

☺ ☺ ☺ ☺ ☺

Andrew, aged three, was very keen on aeroplanes. He was taken to church and seemed to be taking no part in the service. However, when the vicar prayed, "That it may please Thee to give to all nations unity, peace and concord", Andrew remarked aloud to the congregation, 'I've got a concorde too.'

☺ ☺ ☺ ☺ ☺

Lucy, aged five, explaining absence of little brother, aged three: 'He couldn't come to Sunday School today because yesterday he was sick in Tesco's - twice!'

☺ ☺ ☺ ☺ ☺

A new child came to the Sunday School and gazed wonderingly at the superintendent. Finally she asked: 'Do you work here?'

☺ ☺ ☺ ☺ ☺

One wet morning, a Sunday School teacher was trying to get the address of a new small child so that she could enter it in the register.
'And where do you live?' she asked encouragingly.
'At **my** house, of course' said the infant scornfully.
'Which house is that?' persevered the teacher.
'The one with the raindrops on the window,' was the response.

☺ ☺ ☺ ☺ ☺

A child had been taken a walk by his father, and the walk passed through a churchyard. The child noticed a gravestone which read:
>'J. THOMPSON.
>Well done.'

'Does that mean he was cremated?' asked the boy.

(Told by Michael Aspel on 'Child's Play' LWT)

☺ ☺ ☺ ☺ ☺

A certain Canon once had an Emmanuel Primary School in his north-country parish. Emmanuel means 'God with us' and the Canon said to the children, 'How lovely to start your education at Emmanuel! You know what it means, don't you?'

There was no reply, so he tried again.

'What does "goodbye" mean?' (hoping for the answer "God be with you.") Again there was silence until one child ventured, 'It means "Ta ra."'

(Canon T.A. Rockley, Blackburn)

☺ ☺ ☺ ☺ ☺

There was a boy who said he thought the Pharisees were horses. When asked 'Why?' he answered, 'Because Jesus was always saying "Woe!" to them.'

☺ ☺ ☺ ☺ ☺

Looking at a picture of an angel, a four-year old remarked, 'I like angels. Next time we go to the zoo, may we go and see them?'

☺ ☺ ☺ ☺ ☺

1st child, proudly one Saturday:
>"I'm going to Spain next week."

2nd child, not to be outdone:
>"That's nothing. I'm going to see God tomorrow!"

☺ ☺ ☺ ☺ ☺

A-four-year old rushed into church and wanted to sit on the front row near the eagle-shaped lectern. Her mother tried to dissuade her, because she fidgeted and might have been better nearer the back, where they could go out if need be. The child exposulated, 'But I want to sit near the **big crow**!'

☺ ☺ ☺ ☺ ☺

The teacher was telling the Sunday School about Eastern shepherds and how they led their sheep instead of following them. She talked about their dress and showed a picture of a shepherd holding his crook. A small boy gazed wonderingly at it all and then remarked, 'But **my** mummy makes shepherd's pie!

The five-year olds were being told a simplified version of the story of Elisha and the Shunammite woman. The teacher explained that the woman came from a place called Shunem and so was called a Shunammite. 'That's a hard word to say, isn't it?' she said.
'No,' said a small boy airily. 'You only have to think of dynamite and you've got it.'

☺ ☺ ☺ ☺ ☺

On hearing the words of the National Anthem being sung, a little boy asked in a puzzled tone, 'But what does God save our gracious Queen **from?**'

☺ ☺ ☺ ☺ ☺

A nine-year old returned from Sunday School, having heard the parable of the Prodigal Son. Her twin brother had not yet appeared and so the little girl remarked. '**He's** the prodigal son - only he's not come back yet.'

☺ ☺ ☺ ☺ ☺

A church had to use a harmonium when the organ had broken down. The choirboys stared at the new instrument, and one of them asked, 'Are we having that organette thing to sing with?'

☺ ☺ ☺ ☺ ☺

'No-one could make up a story like the Creation, so it must be true.'
(Child's comment in 'The Child Learns' report of a Children's Council Conference held in Hereford in 1965)

☺ ☺ ☺ ☺ ☺

A mother was reading to her 6-year old son from a book about the church which had been written by a friend of theirs. She said to the child, 'You know Miss ..., don't you? Well, she wrote this book.'
The boy gazed thoughtfully at the page for a moment or two, and then he said, 'She's got very neat writing.'

☺ ☺ ☺ ☺ ☺

The Sunday School teacher had said that Lot's wife looked back and was turned into a pillar of salt. A small boy commented, 'My mummy looked back once when she was driving and she turned into a telegraph pole.'

☺ ☺ ☺ ☺ ☺

Two young folk were discussing their confirmation classes.
'We're up to original sin,' said one. 'We're past redemption,' retorted the other.

☺ ☺ ☺ ☺ ☺

The preacher was coming to the end of a powerful sermon on the Exodus.
'At last,' he concluded, thumping the pulpit, 'the Israelites were **free.**'
Whereupon a small shrill voice from the congregation announced, '**I'm** free-and-a-half!'

Vicar's son to mother in church: 'Why does daddy kneel down before he starts to preach?'
Mother: 'He's saying a prayer asking God to help him.'
Son: 'Well, why doesn't He?'

☺ ☺ ☺ ☺ ☺

A little child came home from Sunday School looking very unhappy.
'What's the matter?' asked his mother.
'The teacher said Jesus wants me for a sunbeam - but I want to be an astronaught.'

☺ ☺ ☺ ☺ ☺

Two boys were talking of a Sunday School lesson they had heard about the Devil.
'Do you think there really is a devil?' asked one.
'I doubt it,' said his worldly-wise friend. 'You know how that Father Christmas stuff turned out. It's either your dad or your mum.'

(from BITS & PIECES, Ripon)

☺ ☺ ☺ ☺ ☺

A child asked why we had to pray about different coloured angels. The puzzled parent asked when we did this, and the child replied, 'When we say in church, "Therefore with angels and dark angels..."'

☺ ☺ ☺ ☺ ☺

Auntie had taken her small nephew to look at a church which was rather neglected and in a dusty condition. The boy looked on the generally untidy aspect.
'You did say this was God's house, didn't you?' he asked.
'I did,' replied his aunt.
'Well if I was God,' said the child firmly, 'I should move.'

☺ ☺ ☺ ☺ ☺

'Who's that man?' demanded 3-year-old John, looking at a stained glass window showing Simeon receiving the Child Jesus in His arms.
He was told about Simeon and how he had been waiting a long time to see Jesus.
Now that he had at last seen Him, he was ready to go home happily.
John looked very disbelieving and said, 'Where's his car then?'

☺ ☺ ☺ ☺ ☺

A boy arrived home from Sunday School in tears. 'Teacher said if we wanted to go to heaven we had to put up our hands,' he sobbed.
'But you did that, surely?' said his mother.
'I couldn't,' replied the child, 'Because you said I had to come straight home.'
(retold from 'The Beacon' Barrow-in-Furness)

☺ ☺ ☺ ☺ ☺

A boy asked his grandfather, 'Were you in the Ark?'
'Certainly not!' replied grandfather.
'Why weren't you drowned then?' asked the boy.
(retold from Lancashire magazine)

☺ ☺ ☺ ☺ ☺

An eight-year-old had been to his friend's birthday party. When he returned home his mother asked if he had remembered to thank Mrs Brown for the party before he left.
'No,' replied the boy, 'I did remember what you told me and I was going to say it; but the boy in front of me said it, and Mrs Brown said, "Don't mention it," - so I didn't'. *(Ibid)*

☺ ☺ ☺ ☺ ☺

The small Cub Scout was enthusiastically doing Bob-a-Job week tasks. At one house, he was asked if he would walk the dog. His spelling was not as great as his enthusiasm, and on his Job Card he wrote, 'Taking god for a nice long walk - 10p.

☺ ☺ ☺ ☺ ☺

A little boy had swallowed a coin. His mother was very upset. 'Will someone run for the doctor?' she cried.
'The minister would be better,' said the child. 'I've often heard you say that if anybody can get money out of people he can.'
(re-told from 'KEEP SMILING' by C.W. George [Arthur H. Stockwell])

☺ ☺ ☺ ☺ ☺

The little boy had been listening to his father, a preacher, telling some wonderful stories. After a while he asked, 'Is it true, dad, or are you only preaching?' *(Ibid)*

☺ ☺ ☺ ☺ ☺

On a drawing of a gravestone adorned with a bunch of flowers, a child wrote: 'Here lies Mr Whit and he died in the first world woor in 1160'.

☺ ☺ ☺ ☺ ☺

A small boy was gazing up at the red glow of the sanctuary lamp during what seemed to him to be a very long sermon. Eventually he turned to his mother and said, 'Mummy, when it turns green, can we go?'

☺ ☺ ☺ ☺ ☺

Following a family bereavement, two small children were discussing heaven. 'But what is heaven?' asked one. 'Oh, you'll have to ask granny,' said the other; 'she knows all about it - and she hasn't even been there!'

☺ ☺ ☺ ☺ ☺

'I can't give God any love', remarked a young child. On being asked why not, she replied, 'Because I've given Him all the love I've got.'

☺ ☺ ☺ ☺ ☺

A boy handed in his gift of apples for the Harvest Festival. The vicar thanked him and said, 'I must call and thank your mother for these eight lovely apples.' The child answered, 'Please sir, do you mind thanking her for twelve?'

☺ ☺ ☺ ☺ ☺

A child's eye view of a wedding: 'I have noticed that the bride always changes her mind during the service when she comes to get married. She comes into church with an old man, but she always goes out with a much younger one.'

☺ ☺ ☺ ☺ ☺

An aunt was explaining to her nephew that the preacher on Sunday was coming from the Church Pastoral Aid Society. 'What's that?' said the boy. 'Is it a society for hard up farm-workers?'

☺ ☺ ☺ ☺ ☺

A young friend of a Confirmation candidate in Suffolk was preparing to go to the Confirmation Service. She asked her mother; 'What shall I wear to Natasha's cremation?' *(Re-told from Church Times 'Portugal Street Diary')*

☺ ☺ ☺ ☺ ☺

A minister had been to visit a dying man. On his return his little daughter asked; 'Has Mr .... gone to Jesus yet? The minister replied somewhat absently, 'No, but he's on his way.'

The child immediately went outside and gazed at the heavens. After a while she came back indoors and remarked, 'Well, I can't see him anywhere about.'

☺ ☺ ☺ ☺ ☺

One of the choristers at Carlisle Cathedral must have found inspiration in the title of the anthem for Ash Wednesday, thinks Church Times reader Mr John Barratt, who saw inscribed in the dust on an Assistant Organist's car: "Wash me throughly..." *(Church Times 'Portugal Street Diary')*

A friend of the family had died and mother had said she must get a condolence card to send.

'What's a condolence card?' asked her young daughter.

'It's a card you send when someone has died,' replied the mother.

After a pause for thought, the child asked, 'Where do you send it?'

☺ ☺ ☺ ☺ ☺

b) MISHEARD

A child wanted to know what tinthemies were. She said that the vicar had said that God made heaven and earth and all the tinthemies. (All that in them is.)

☺ ☺ ☺ ☺ ☺

'We can sing, full though we be', sang a child for 'Weak and sinful though we be.'

☺ ☺ ☺ ☺ ☺

'What's a bloodless coldly?' asked Jean, having sung in Good King Wenceslas, 'Freeze thy blood less coldly.'

☺ ☺ ☺ ☺ ☺

Various versions of the Lord's Prayer have come from children's lips, or in writing including:

'Our Father, Harold be Thy Name,'
'Our Father, how d' you know my name?'
'Our Father, down by our lane.

'Lead us not into Trent Station.'
'Are daily dred'
'On urf has in even.'

☺ ☺ ☺ ☺ ☺

'The kettles are lowing,' sang Roger in "Away in a Manger."

☺ ☺ ☺ ☺ ☺

'All things bright and beautiful. All teachers great and small,' sang a small girl; while a gardener's daughter sang, 'Aubretias great and small.' *(Church Teacher)*

☺ ☺ ☺ ☺ ☺

At the Last Supper Jesus and the Disciples ate unleaded bread

☺ ☺ ☺ ☺ ☺

The Wise Men offered Gold, Frank Instance and Mirth

(Scripture Union 'Daily Notes')

At the wedding reception they said we could have prophets ear'oles with cream or fruit salad.

☺ ☺ ☺ ☺ ☺

The teacher asked the children what St Matthew did for a living. One child answered that he kept a cab-rank. Seeing the teacher's puzzlement, he added, 'But you said last week that he collected taxis, sir.' *(Church Teacher)*

☺ ☺ ☺ ☺ ☺

The hymn, 'Jesus bids us shine first of all for Him. Well he sees and knows it if our light is dim,' was rendered by one young voice as, 'Well he sees our noses if our light is dim.' *(Ibid)*

☺ ☺ ☺ ☺ ☺

'Surely to goodness Thy mercy shall follow me all the days of my life...' was a child's misheard version of the 23rd Psalm. *(Ibid)*

☺ ☺ ☺ ☺ ☺

A small boy had been taken to church for some time, and his mother felt he was taking no interest in the proceedings, nor listening to anything which was going on. She was about to give up when her sister took the child to Liverpool one day. On seeing the river he asked what it was called.
'You won't have heard it yet,' replied his aunt, 'but it is called the River Mersey.'
'Course I've heard of it,' said the boy scornfully. 'We have it in church every Sunday.'
'In church?' echoed his mystified aunt.
'Yes, the man says "Lord have mersey upon us" every week.'

☺ ☺ ☺ ☺ ☺

c) CHRISTMAS

A child told his teacher that he knew the name of one of the shepherds who went to the manger at Bethlehem on the first Christmas night. When the teacher said that no-one knew the name of any of the shepherds, the child persisted, 'But we do, because we sing about him. He's called Ted.' The teacher was even more puzzled until the child sang, 'While shepherds watched their flocks by night, all see Ted on the ground...' *(Church Teacher)*

☺ ☺ ☺ ☺ ☺

Anne Arnott, in "Wife to the Archbishop" (The life story of Jean Coggan, published by Mowbrays), tells of a Yorkshire Sunday School class hearing the story of the first Christmas night. They were very interested when they heard that there was no room in the inn for Mary and Joseph.

Many Yorkshire people, among others, prepare for their holidays very methodically and, bearing this in mind, one boy commented solemnly, 'Ah blame Joseph. He should have booked.'

☺ ☺ ☺ ☺ ☺

A two-year-old was delighted to be one of the shepherds in the church Nativity play. He was so small as to be hardly visible among the other children on the stage; but the parents could see his crook which kept rising higher and higher above the heads of the taller actors.

Later it transpired that young Richard, bored with having to stand there and say nothing, was doing his best to bring down the decorations with his crook. Fortunately, he did not succeed.

☺ ☺ ☺ ☺ ☺

In a Nativity play, a boy was disappointed at not getting the part of Joseph. Instead he was cast as the innkeeper. When Joseph asked him if there was any room, the innkeeper wrecked the whole play, by saying, 'Yes, of course; come in.'

☺ ☺ ☺ ☺ ☺

The teacher was trying to get the class to see that there were many things to be thankful for at Christmas as well as receiving presents. She asked the children for other suggestions, and one boy said, 'I'm thankful I'm not a turkey.'

☺ ☺ ☺ ☺ ☺

Child to Sunday School teacher on Christmas morning in church: 'Ooh miss, I forgot your Christmas card.' Then, after a pause, 'Never mind, you can have it next year.'

☺ ☺ ☺ ☺ ☺

d) CHILDREN'S PRAYERS

Dear God, please look after mummy and daddy and nanny and see they don't die before I'm grown up. Please see daddy does not crash in the car.

☺ ☺ ☺ ☺ ☺

Dear God, thank you for letting mummy cook the dinner without burning her fingers. Thank you for the dinner we eat every day that nourishes us and makes us grow so we can eat it.

☺ ☺ ☺ ☺ ☺

O God, thank you for the taxi drivers for giving us rides when the car has broken down.

☺ ☺ ☺ ☺ ☺

Dear God, please help the grass to grow, the sun to shine and birds to sing, may the good thrive and the bad wither, may babies sleep and houses stand.

☺ ☺ ☺ ☺ ☺

The parents of a small girl who had just learnt to talk were telling her about the need to say grace before meals.
'Don't you want to say Thank You to Jesus,' suggested father, a vicar. Whereupon the child looked up and said laconically, 'Ta, Jee.'

A Poetic Prayer: God is a very nice man,
                    So is Jesus too,
                    I have not yet see you,
                    But I hope I do.

☺ ☺ ☺ ☺ ☺

e) COMMENTS ON THE CLERGY

The new vicar came into the Sunday School, clad in his cassock, which caused much wonderment among the children, many never having seen him thus at close quarters before. His cassock was obviously a dress to them and they could not reconcile this with his deep voice.
Finally one puzzled youngster whispered to his teacher, 'Is it a man?'

☺ ☺ ☺ ☺ ☺

A Bishop was paying his second visit to a church within a few months. The choir was told and the youngsters firmly admonished to be on their best behaviour. 'But who is the Bishop?' asked one choirboy.
'Don't you remember?' said one of the adults. 'We saw him arrive last time, when he came into this vestry by mistake. He was carrying a suitcase....'
Light dawned on the boy. 'Oh, you mean that chap in tights?' he said. (The Bishop had been wearing gaiters).

☺ ☺ ☺ ☺ ☺

A little girl was taken to church where there was a surpliced choir. The church she had been used to did not have a choir and she stared aghast at all those white-robed people. 'They're not **all** going to preach, are they?' she gasped.

☺ ☺ ☺ ☺ ☺

A young teenager was asked how you would tell a Bishop from the other clergy. The answer was: 'He would have a kind face and hairy hands. Red hair and a beard. He would have a chain round his neck. He has a robe and a sort of train. His collar would be back to front. He has a sort of crown. His hat is called a mighter.' *(Church Teacher)*

☺ ☺ ☺ ☺ ☺

An archdeacon had been explaining the functions of various church dignitaries to a class of children. He included the bishop, his crook, mitre, pectoral cross etc. At the end, when he asked the class, 'What is an archdeacon?' he got the reply, 'Something that hangs round the bishop's neck.'
(Told by the Rt. Rev. Roy Williamson when Archdeacon of Nottingham)

☺ ☺ ☺ ☺ ☺

A Bishop, robed and carrying his crook, came across to the vicarage for a meal after the service. The vicar's small son opened the door to him, and in a voice of great surprise, called out, 'Here's Little Bo-peep come to see you, daddy.'

☺ ☺ ☺ ☺ ☺

The son of a newly appointed Bishop asked his father, 'Daddy, will you now be a Very Rev. or a Right Rev.?' to which the Bishop replied, with a grin, 'A very right Rev.: always have been!'

☺ ☺ ☺ ☺ ☺

A Bishop was going to his enthronement service, and the procession was watched by a large crowd as it neared the cathedral.
'What's going on?' asked someone in the crowd. To which a child replied, 'Somebody's going to be crowned, I think.'

☺ ☺ ☺ ☺ ☺

The Vicar's small son became bored with his father's sermon: so he stood up on the pew and, before anybody could stop him, called out, 'that's enough for this week, daddy.'

☺ ☺ ☺ ☺ ☺

A Vicar's daughter was carefully instructed that, when the Bishop came to visit, she must remember to call him 'My Lord'.
The Bishop duly arrived, and kindly asked the child how old she was. Nervously she answered, 'My God, I'm seven.'

☺ ☺ ☺ ☺ ☺

The curate's small son was becoming very bored with the vicar's address. Finally be looked up at the vicar and in a penetrating voice asked, 'When's the last hymn?'

At the end of the service, the priest knelt in the sanctuary for a silent prayer, and a child's voice piped up: 'Is he counting for Hide and Seek?'

Rev. J. McKegney: retold from Church Times 'Portugal Street Diary')

☺ ☺ ☺ ☺ ☺

The Bishop of Lichfield had been wondering what children imagine when they hear that the Bishop is coming. 'Oh-h' he heard one child say, 'look, it's just a MAN.' *(Church Times, 'Portugal Street Diary')*

☺ ☺ ☺ ☺ ☺

In the diocese of St Albans during Lent an informal family service was proceeding while the incumbent was away on a pilgrimage. The children were asked to look around and suggest what the Church was giving up for Lent. According to the Diocesan Magazine 'See Round', one toddler swiftly suggested, 'The Vicar'. *(Ibid)*

☺ ☺ ☺ ☺ ☺

Child's eye view of a bishop: 'He wore a gold cape with a hat to match, with two bookmarkers hanging down the back.' *(Ibid)*

☺ ☺ ☺ ☺ ☺

When the children of a church infants' school were asked to suggest suitable presents for different people, one child thought that the appropriate gift for the vicar would be 'a proper shirt.'

(Rev'd Peter Godden: Church Times 'Portugal Street Diary')

☺ ☺ ☺ ☺ ☺

f) THE COLLECTION

The vicar observed a young child putting 2p. in the alms box at the back of the church. He patted her head, commendingly, at which she retorted, 'But nothing came out!'

☺ ☺ ☺ ☺ ☺

Another child, observing the collecting bag as it went round during a hymn, asked afterwards, 'Why do they take the collection in half an oven glove?'

☺ ☺ ☺ ☺ ☺

Two children both put their hands into the collection bag as it came round. At the end of the service, one said to the other, 'I got 10p. How much did you get?'

☺ ☺ ☺ ☺ ☺

g) PHONETIC SPELLINGS
From a list of things seen in a church:
> Carpits, Raidyaters, Alter, Trumpits,
> Candlestikes, Varses, Brics, gats, handls,
> notice bord, cushon.

From certain Proper names:
> Jowsef, Joshept, Jerermiya, Glliath,
> Nebercunezur.

☺ ☺ ☺ ☺ ☺

h) VERBAL ANSWERS
The teacher was explaining that the Church is made up of people. She used the device CH--CH and asked what was missing to complete the word, hoping to follow the answer with, 'Yes, You Are.' But the effect was ruined by one child who answered that what was missing was 'E R, miss.'

☺ ☺ ☺ ☺ ☺

A teacher was trying to explain the Trinity as being three in one. By way of illustration, she asked the children for all the words they could think of beginning with T R I.
They came out with 'triangle', 'tricycle', 'tripod', etc.
When the list seemed exhausted, the teacher said, 'I don't think there are any more...' and was about to explain that these things were not each three separate things, but one thing with three parts. She was interrupted.
'There's another T R I word, miss,' said a bright boy. 'What about trifle?'
'Ah,' said the teacher, somewhat non-plussed. 'Now that isn't a three-in-one sort of word.'
'But it is, miss,' persisted the boy. 'It's sponge cake and jelly and custard, all in one dish; three in one, like you said.'

☺ ☺ ☺ ☺ ☺

'What are sins of omission?' asked the teacher.
After a puzzled silence, one boy ventured, 'The sins we should have committed - and didn't.

☺ ☺ ☺ ☺ ☺

At a Family Service a minister held up three cards bearing the words 'Eden', 'Gethsemane' and 'Easter'. He asked what they all had in common, no doubt hoping for the answer 'gardens'.
He was somewhat taken aback when a child answered, 'They're all cheeses.'

(re-written from Church Times 'Portugal Street Diary')

☺ ☺ ☺ ☺ ☺

A child described a parable as 'a heavenly story with no earthly meaning.'

('Keep Smiling' - C.W. George [Arthur H. Stockwell])

☺ ☺ ☺ ☺ ☺

Teacher: 'What is the outward and visible sign of Baptism?'
Child: 'The baby, sir'. *(Ibid)*

☺ ☺ ☺ ☺ ☺

The class was learning the names of the various parts of the church. On being shown the altar-rail, where the priest blessed the children at Holy Communion, one boy suggested, 'Is it called the blessing-bar?'

☺ ☺ ☺ ☺ ☺

A teacher was teaching in a draughty classroom, when a child came in leaving the door wide open.
'And who was born in a barn?' asked the teacher.
Instantly came the reply, 'Jesus, sir.' *(re-told from St Stephen-by-Saltash Parish News).*

☺ ☺ ☺ ☺ ☺

SHORT ANSWERS:

What is the Agnus Dei?	A lady composer of church music.
What are Fast Days?	Days when you have to eat in a hurry.
Who was Joan of Arc?	Noah's wife.
What is a layman?	Someone who stays in bed on Sunday mornings.
What is parsimony?	The vicar's salary.

(Knutsford Parish Magazine)

☺ ☺ ☺ ☺ ☺

The children were asked to draw someone famous. Some efforts were recognisable, others less so. One effort was very puzzling.
'Who is that?' enquired the teacher.
'It's God,' was the answer.
'But we don't know what God looks like,' said the teacher, to which the artist replied, 'You will do as soon as I've finished this.'

☺ ☺ ☺ ☺ ☺

The Vicar went into the day school where a religious lesson was in progress.
'Who broke down the walls of Jericho?' he asked.
'It wasn't me, sir,' said one boy, at which the vicar turned to the teacher in some surprise. 'He is an honest boy,' said the teacher. 'I do not doubt him.'
Disgustedly the vicar went to the Director of Religious Education, and was amazed when she supported both the boy and the teacher.
Later the vicar told the story to his Church Council, at which one of the members said, 'Let's pay for the damage and charge it to upkeep.'

What did Noah say when the rain stopped? - 'Ark'.

(Knutsford Parish Magazine)

☺ ☺ ☺ ☺ ☺

The class had been learning about the flight of Mary, Joseph and the Child Jesus into Egypt. They were asked to draw a picture of it. One child drew Mary on a donkey and Joseph walking alongside, with a big black dot between them. The teacher asked about the dot.
'It's the flea,' said the child. 'The Bible said Joseph was to take Mary and the young Child and flee into Egypt.'

☺ ☺ ☺ ☺ ☺

A Sunday School teacher was trying to differentiate between John the Baptist and John the Evangelist in the minds of the older children.
'We all know about St John the Baptist,' she began, 'but who is the other St John?' Silence, until one child ventured, 'Is it St John the Ambulance?'

☺ ☺ ☺ ☺ ☺

Asked, on the Sunday after Ascension Day, what had been the special name of the previous Thursday, one boy replied, 'Essential Day'.

☺ ☺ ☺ ☺ ☺

One Whitsunday, the children in church were being given a children's talk which included a lighted candle to illustrate flame, and a loud blast on the organ to simulate the rushing mighty wind. It was all very realistic, so the adults thought. When the children went out into their Sunday School groups, the Whitsun story was told them in more detail. Building up the expectant atmosphere, the leader explained how the disciples waited for the gift of the Holy Spirit. 'Then, on the tenth day,' she concluded, 'they heard something very surprising. What was it?' A bright three-year old immediately volunteered, 'Big noise on the organ.'

☺ ☺ ☺ ☺ ☺

Bishop: 'Well, son, which part of the service did you like best?'
Small boy: 'The end.'

('Share' - Chester Diocese)

☺ ☺ ☺ ☺ ☺

Following a lesson on the Beatitudes, a mother asked her children if they could remember any of the people whom Jesus had said were blessed. Her youngest son replied, 'Blessed are the prosecuted.'

(Rev. G. Brown)

☺ ☺ ☺ ☺ ☺

i) WRITTEN ANSWERS

Requiring the answer 'water' the children were asked what was the essential thing to be put in the font at baptism. One child wrote, 'the plug.'

☺ ☺ ☺ ☺ ☺

The class was asked to write two facts which they knew about certain Biblical characters. One child, writing of Solomon, put, '(1) He had lots of wives. (2) He was very wise.'

☺ ☺ ☺ ☺ ☺

The paralytic was borne of four. This means he had three brothers born at the same time. *(Church Teacher' article by Lilian M Naylor)*

☺ ☺ ☺ ☺ ☺

Our Lord cured divers diseases. This means he cured all kinds of people including lepers and divers. *(Ibid)*

☺ ☺ ☺ ☺ ☺

Elizabeth knows that Mary is to be the Mother of God, and runs out to meet her saying the Magna Carter. *(Ibid)*

☺ ☺ ☺ ☺ ☺

On the birth of John the Baptist: - 'Zacharias did not believe and he remained dumb until it came to pass. Elizabeth was very glad at this.' *(Ibid)*

☺ ☺ ☺ ☺ ☺

Who are the three Persons of the Holy Trinity?
    - Vicar, Bishop, Choir.
    - God, Vicar, Bishop. *(Ibid)*

☺ ☺ ☺ ☺ ☺

What are the outward signs in Baptism?
    - Babies. *(Ibid)*

☺ ☺ ☺ ☺ ☺

When we hear these words what should we reply:
'Lift up your hearts'. - And I'll lift mine. *(Ibid)*

☺ ☺ ☺ ☺ ☺

Write out the words of the Commandment which tells us how we should treat our parents.
'Do not boss them about and swear at them. Thou shalt do no murder.' *(Ibid)*

☺ ☺ ☺ ☺ ☺

Who said, 'Jesus, Master, have mercy on us?'
- Noah, when the flood came.

(Chester Diocese - quoted in 'Church Teacher')

☺ ☺ ☺ ☺ ☺

Who betrayed Christ with a kiss? - Judas's chariot. *(Ibid)*

☺ ☺ ☺ ☺ ☺

Ending to the story of the Prodigal Son: '... he saw his son coming and ran and fell on his neck and nearly broke it.' *(Ibid)*

☺ ☺ ☺ ☺ ☺

Where did John baptize Jesus?
- In the Suez Canal. *(Ibid)*

☺ ☺ ☺ ☺ ☺

What were the promises your godparents made for you at baptism? - I shall defend the devil and all his works. *(Ibid)*

☺ ☺ ☺ ☺ ☺

I think in fights or quarrels God tells the one that is wrong to lose.

(Ibid)

☺ ☺ ☺ ☺ ☺

The devil is a sort of little voice in your stomach. *(Ibid)*

☺ ☺ ☺ ☺ ☺

A child wrote: I asked by mother what God is like, but she did not know. Father did not know and teacher did not know. I think that if I had lived as long as my mother, my father and my teacher, I would know what God is like.

(Rev'd. A. Carver)

☺ ☺ ☺ ☺ ☺

Noah took two of every animal into the ark, including his wife.'

☺ ☺ ☺ ☺ ☺

Q: Who asked, 'Which of these three proved neighbour to the man who fell among the robbers?'
A: The good saint Maritain. *(Church Teacher)*

☺ ☺ ☺ ☺ ☺

'God rewarded Elizabeth by giving her a child, and a holy child at that.' *(Ibid)*

☺ ☺ ☺ ☺ ☺

If Tom is short for Thomas and Matt is short for Matthew, is Luke short for Lucozade? (question from an 8 year old).

☺ ☺ ☺ ☺ ☺

The Prodigal Son (in a nutshell) from an 11 year old:
When their father dies each 2 of them could have his money but one of them said I want mine now. He had it, spent it, and then his father took him back and gave a party. *(Chester Diocese) (Children's exams)*

☺ ☺ ☺ ☺ ☺

Pastor of an evangelical church, describing his vision for a new church building:
"We will invite local people in, and offer the community what they need. There will be a mother and toddler group, with experienced mothers to teach potty training. We will need a big building, because we will be flooded out!"

☺ ☺ ☺ ☺ ☺

Q: - What miracle teaches us to say thank you?
A: - The wedding. *(Ibid)*

☺ ☺ ☺ ☺ ☺

Q: - Write down something Jesus did by the seashore.
A: - Piked his disciples. *(Ibid)*

☺ ☺ ☺ ☺ ☺

Q: - On what day did Jesus give the Last Supper?
A: - He said it on Monday Thursday. (Also Mourn Day Thursday). *(Ibid)*

☺ ☺ ☺ ☺ ☺

Q: - Why is the first day of the week important to a Christian?
A: - Because on a Sunday you're forgiven your sins, so on a Monday you start all over again. *(Ibid)*

☺ ☺ ☺ ☺ ☺

Q: - What expression did Jesus use to describe how hard it is for the rich to enter heaven?
A: - It is easier for a caramel to go through the eye of a needle.

☺ ☺ ☺ ☺ ☺

End of a written prayer: '... the fellowsheep of the Holy Spirit be a monster and remain with us.' *(Ibid)*

☺ ☺ ☺ ☺ ☺

Variation on the Creed: 'I believe in God the Father, Almighty, Maker of heavenly earth.' *(Ibid)*

☺ ☺ ☺ ☺ ☺

Answers from pupils in 1987 Religious Studies exams:
1) Jews are not allowed to eat birds that pray.
2) A shofar drives cars at a wedding.
3) The Muslim name for God is Alan.
4) Perjury is somewhere Roman Catholics believe you go when you die.
5) The Bible had to be translated into English because the Romans spoke Greek.
6) Roman Catholics allow divorce if the marriage is dull and void.
7) Paul and Silas were persecuted because they were said to be blastformers.
8) Ruth was gleaming in the field.
9) Yom Kippur is a fish dish which Jews eat on Fridays.

('Together')

j) DEFINITIONS

(i) About God

God would look like a big grey cloud, with a big face formed out in it, a stern, long face. *(Taken from 'The Child Learns' (report of Children's Council Conference at Hereford, 1965).*

☺ ☺ ☺ ☺ ☺

God might have done miracles like Jesus if he had been alive then, but no-one else could. *(Ibid)*

☺ ☺ ☺ ☺ ☺

He let the people drown in the flood to let them know they'd been naughty. *(Ibid)*

☺ ☺ ☺ ☺ ☺

God's got sort of cloths for his clothes, and he's got a sort of beard. *(Ibid)*

☺ ☺ ☺ ☺ ☺

Our Farther lives in the holy cherch. He is like a man. *(Ibid)*

☺ ☺ ☺ ☺ ☺

If you saw God it would be just a voice with no-one owning it. *(Ibid)*

☺ ☺ ☺ ☺ ☺

God did miracles in those days because people were badder and God wanted to make the world better. *(Ibid)*

☺ ☺ ☺ ☺ ☺

If you saw God he'd look like a good man and be all orangey. *(Ibid)*

☺ ☺ ☺ ☺ ☺

Moses was a good Christian but there aren't enough about today for God to do miracles. *(Ibid)*

I amagain God to be a very hard working man, thinking of what else there is to make our world even more beautiful. He is a Christian who helps people that need help. *(Ibid)*

☺ ☺ ☺ ☺ ☺

God looks to me like a fairly old man but still has a lot of power left.

(Ibid)

☺ ☺ ☺ ☺ ☺

God is the only man of his kind I am sure. He is fairly tall I think.

(Ibid)

☺ ☺ ☺ ☺ ☺

I think that God is shaped like a human being because in the Bible it said he made Adem to look like himself. I amagine he as a long beard due to his great age. *(Ibid)*

☺ ☺ ☺ ☺ ☺

God is in heaven because he has always done right. The devil is in hell because he has done wrong. *(Ibid)*

ii) ABOUT HEAVEN and other definitions

Heaven is where people go when they are dead. It is covered with soil. *(Ibid)*

☺ ☺ ☺ ☺ ☺

In heaven is God he is beeter than Jesus. *(Ibid)*

☺ ☺ ☺ ☺ ☺

Heaven as I think it is, is just above the clouds. It is a field of buttercups which has a wall round it. God is sitting in the middle of it with Angels sitting round him on the grass. *(Ibid)*

☺ ☺ ☺ ☺ ☺

Heaven is a place where planits are. *(Ibid)*

☺ ☺ ☺ ☺ ☺

Heaven is the best place to live but some people just think it is very horrable. They do not want to die. But you do not feel a thing. *(Ibid)*

☺ ☺ ☺ ☺ ☺

You can't get to heaven in a space-ship because it's invisible.

(Ibid)

☺ ☺ ☺ ☺ ☺

Heaven I think is up to the sky or higher. I thought it was big enough for about two hundred men to fit their. In heaven their is nothing to hold a man to the ground. Heaven is, I think, a place that pecular plants and fruits grow in red soil. You could probably float there. *(Ibid)*

Heaven is an empty space where Christians live. In this space there is a chair for God to sit on. *(Ibid)*

☺ ☺ ☺ ☺ ☺

Heaven is on earth. Not up in the sky as most people think. Heaven is God's Kingdom and God's Kingdom is the world so the world must be heaven. *(Ibid)*

☺ ☺ ☺ ☺ ☺

Heaven is a misty place where they sleep out at night... there are stachoows and steps all over the place with a great big sigament Book. *(Ibid)*

☺ ☺ ☺ ☺ ☺

I think that heaven is a great nation a-bove the clouds has no houses or a roof. No wall around it just a big gate where every-body is honest and wont sneak in or out. There are jobs for every-body so that they will be able to live by what they earn. There is no noise in heaven. I think every person is heaven dresses in cloaks made of white cloth and wear sandel on their feet. *(Ibid)*

☺ ☺ ☺ ☺ ☺

Heaven is about eight miles up. *(Ibid)*

☺ ☺ ☺ ☺ ☺

Jesus came down from heaven - you couldn't get to heaven in a spaceship because of the millions and millions and millions and millions of years it takes to get up there - I don't think Jesus could be come all that way down - ooh! *(Ibid)*

☺ ☺ ☺ ☺ ☺

Heaven is above the stars, so I've heard. *(Ibid)*

☺ ☺ ☺ ☺ ☺

A Bishop was visiting a parish and noticed various posters up referring to 'The Bishop's Visitation'. When he went into the Sunday School, he asked the children if they knew what a Visitation was. One child's definition was, 'A plague sent by God.' *(Church Times)*

PART II
THE LIGHTER SIDE OF ADULT CHURCH LIFE

a) General

A disgruntled man was commenting on the various new versions of the Bible which are about. 'If King James' English was good enough for St Paul,' he said, 'then it's good enough for me.'

☺ ☺ ☺ ☺ ☺

Some monks were only allowed to speak once in every four years. At the end of four years, one of them said, 'I don't like the porridge we get here.' Four years later another agreed, 'I don't like it either.' After a further period of four years had passed, the monastery cook said, 'If I hear any more of this constant complaining, I shall resign.'

☺ ☺ ☺ ☺ ☺

A certain Methodist church felt it was wrong to pray for fine weather for their own events. The nearby Baptist church nearly always prayed for fine weather, and they usually got it. So the Methodists simply took the precaution of arranging their outdoor events on the same days as the Baptists.

☺ ☺ ☺ ☺ ☺

A churchwarden was standing outside the church trying to encourage more people to come in.
'Won't you come and join us,' he said to one man.
'No thanks,' was the reply, 'I've got enough troubles of my own.'

☺ ☺ ☺ ☺ ☺

A lady was gazing at a War Memorial outside a church when the vicar came up.
'What is this?' she asked.
'It's a memorial to all those who died in the Services,' he replied.
'Oh, did they die in the Morning Service or the Evening Service?' asked the lady.

☺ ☺ ☺ ☺ ☺

From Survival Rules for Choristers Never close your eyes when singing, in case the choir moves off in procession leaving you behind.
(from 'The Cassock Pocket Book') (RSCM).

☺ ☺ ☺ ☺ ☺

Hint for a new verger: Make the collection **sound** like a collection. This encourages generosity and lets the organist know where you are.
('The Cassock Pocket Book' - by Gordon Reynolds). (RSCM)

Organist's Ear-view '...there was the sound of distant sea-lions flopping as the congregation knelt.' *(Ibid)*

☺ ☺ ☺ ☺ ☺

11th Commandment: The wife of an enthusiastic church councillor suggested that the 11th Commandment should be, 'Thou shalt not Committ-ee'.

☺ ☺ ☺ ☺ ☺

A weathered old sea-captain was asked how he knew when to sit, stand or kneel during the new Alternative Service Book services. He replied, 'I just sits in the stern and I rise and fall with the tide.'

☺ ☺ ☺ ☺ ☺

A vicar was trying to help his people to see the difference between fact and faith. He said, 'That I am standing in this pulpit is fact; that you are sitting in the pews is also fact; but that any of you is listening to what I am saying is an act of faith.'

☺ ☺ ☺ ☺ ☺

A lonely traveller fell over a cliff one night. He managed to grab hold of a bush on the way down, and hung there in the darkness shouting, 'Is anyone down there?'
'Yes,' replied a voice. 'I am here. Let yourself go and trust me. I am God.'
After a long silence, the traveller called out, 'Is anybody else down there?'
(Told by Rt. Rev. J.S. Habgood when Bishop of Durham)

☺ ☺ ☺ ☺ ☺

An old man in Nottingham was listening to a Lesson about St Paul's visits to Derbe, Lystra and Iconium. Afterwards he said, 'It seems Paul visited here, for that Lesson said he was at Derby, Leicester - and I suppose Iconium is an old name for Nottingham'.
(re-told from 'Keep Smiling' - by C.W. George [Arthur H Stockwell])

☺ ☺ ☺ ☺ ☺

Two ladies were talking about the annual Methodist Conferences.
'Why do they have these conferences?' asked one.
'They meet and exchange sermons,' her friend replied. 'Well they don't do it very fairly,' answered the other. 'Our minister comes back with a worse set each time.' *(Ibid)*

☺ ☺ ☺ ☺ ☺

C. H. Spurgeon was once asked if it was possible to be a Christian and to be in a brass band. He replied, 'I see no difficulty about it. But if the man in the brass band plays the trombone and practises at home, it will be hard for the man next door to be a Christian.' *(Ibid)*

According to the Saddleworth, Oldham, parish magazine. 'A man accused of stealing candles from Carlisle Cathedral had his case temporarily adjourned when the court heard he had wax in his ear.
(Church Times - Portugal Street Diary)

☺ ☺ ☺ ☺ ☺

An ordinand in retreat went out for a walk in the town. Unfortunately, he met the Bishop who wanted to know what he was doing away from the retreat. 'The Lord told me I must go and do some shopping,' was the reply. The Bishop raised an eyebrow. 'It's a pity the Lord didn't tell you it is half day closing today,' he said.

☺ ☺ ☺ ☺ ☺

'I often think that the pianos we have in our churches and church halls are what the Psalmist was prophetically referring to when he talked of the instruments of ten strings.' *(Prof. Rowland Moss, Salford University)*

☺ ☺ ☺ ☺ ☺

A generous man was wont to give large donations to his local church, although he never attended its services or contributed in any other way.
A newcomer to the parish remarked that it must be wonderful to have such a pillar of the church living in the town.
The vicar's comment was that the benefactor was not so much a pillar, but more of a flying buttress - giving support from outside.

☺ ☺ ☺ ☺ ☺

An article in the **Royal School of Church Music's Journal 'Church Music'** about shortages of organists was spotted by the national press, with the result that various dramatic headlines appeared: 'Top organist pipes up about shortage', 'Riddle of vanishing organists', 'Shortage of notes hits organs', and 'There's a famine at the organ.' *(RSCM)*

☺ ☺ ☺ ☺ ☺

Spoonerisms
a) Sidesman to lady entering church: May I sow you to a sheet, madam? (Church Times).
b) The Vicar knows every crook and nanny in the parish.
(Miss E Thomas Church Times)
c) Here beginneth the first actor of chaps. *(Rev. C R de Lyons-Pike)*
d) From death's dead string, thy servants free. *(Church Times)*

☺ ☺ ☺ ☺ ☺

Vicar gazing at a new church, built in a very modern style: I don't know whether to pray in it, at it, or for it.

The Roman Catholic priest was hospital visiting and saw a list in the Sister's office with the names of the patients on it. After each name was a small 'r.c' or 'p'. He was delighted that the majority had 'r.c' after their names. When he expressed his surprise to the sister that so many were of his faith, she replied, 'But that's not their religion. It's the breakfast list, and it means that 23 want rice crispies and 3 want porridge.'

☺ ☺ ☺ ☺ ☺

King James I is said to have commented on the works of John Donne: 'Dr Donne's verses are like the peace of God; they pass all understanding.'

☺ ☺ ☺ ☺ ☺

Mark Twain: To be good is noble, but to teach others to be good is nobler - and less trouble.'

☺ ☺ ☺ ☺ ☺

The Vicar's Motto: When in charge, ponder.
When in trouble, delegate.
When in doubt, mumble.
(seen in a Vicar's vestry). (Origin unknown).

☺ ☺ ☺ ☺ ☺

The very nervous bridegroom, when asked in the wedding service, 'Wilt thou take this woman to be thy lawful wedded wife?' replied tremblingly, 'I wilt'.

☺ ☺ ☺ ☺ ☺

A Bishop was staying in a hotel, and the new page boy was being sent up to his room.
'What shall I say?' asked the boy nervously.
'Just knock on the door, and when he answers, say, 'It's the boy, m'Lord', he was told.
In great trepidation, the boy went up, rehearsing his little speech all the way.
He then knocked on the door and said, 'It's the Lord, m'boy'.

☺ ☺ ☺ ☺ ☺

A British girl took her American boyfriend to church one Sunday morning. During the service, the vicar read out the Banns of Marriage, ending with 'This is for the third time of asking.
At which, the perplexed American whispered loudly to his girl, 'Say, how many times does a fella have to ask a girl in this country?'

☺ ☺ ☺ ☺ ☺

A man went fishing and had not returned the following day, a Sunday. His worried wife gave a note to the vicar, asking for prayers for her husband. The note read: 'James, having gone to sea, his wife requires the prayers of the congregation that he may return safely.'
Unfortunately the note was read out thus: 'James, having gone to see his wife, requires the prayers of the congregation that he may return safely.'

☺ ☺ ☺ ☺ ☺

A theological student had to write two essays, one on the Holy Spirit and the other on the Devil. He tackled the one on the Holy spirit first, and found that it took up so much time, that he was unable to start the second essay. In order to show that he had not forgotten it, he wrote, 'I've no time for the Devil.'

☺ ☺ ☺ ☺ ☺

'What are you going to call your new baby girl?' asked a neighbour as the family set off for the Baptism.
'Hazel', replied the proud mother.
'What?' gasped the neighbour. 'With all the lovely saints' names there are, why do you have to call your baby after a nut?'

☺ ☺ ☺ ☺ ☺

A visiting preacher was being entertained for the weekend at a local farm. The farmer killed a fowl for his guest, who appreciated it so much that there was none left for Sunday. So the farmer killed another bird for Sunday lunch. On Monday morning, as the preacher was leaving, he saw the cockerel proudly crowing from the gate-post.
'He seems very pleased with himself,' remarked the preacher.
'And well he might,' said the farmer, 'for he's now got two sons in the ministry.'

☺ ☺ ☺ ☺ ☺

An angry curate 'phoned the Bishop's house intending to spill out his wrath on the Bishop's secretary. He began his tirade as soon as the phone was picked up at the other end.
'Do you know whom you are addressing?' said the voice of the Bishop himself, as soon as he could get a word in.
'Do you know who is talking to you?' asked the rather deflated curate.
'Not yet,' replied the Bishop.
'Thank goodness,' said the curate, hastily putting the 'phone down.

☺ ☺ ☺ ☺ ☺

'Will you marry me?' asked the ardent young man.
'I fear I can never marry,' replied the girl. 'I am a somnambulist.'
'But that's no problem,' laughed the young man. 'I'm a Methodist; you can come to my church on Sunday mornings, and we'll both go to your place on Sunday evenings.'

☺☺☺☺☺

A clergyman in New Mexico used to rush down to the railway station every day to watch the Southern Pacific train go by. When upbraided for his eccentricity, he replied, 'I love watching that train. It's the only thing that goes through this town that I don't have to push.'

☺☺☺☺☺

The Vicarage was sited between the church and a convent. It had a lovely rose garden, of which the vicar was very proud.
One day, a parishioner came to him and said, 'You don't seem to have as many roses this year, vicar.'
'No,' he answered, 'they have suffered from the Black Death.'
'Whatever is that?' questioned the parishioner.
The vicar nodded towards the convent. 'Nuns with scissors,' he said, briefly.

b) MAINLY CLERICAL
A Bishop was visiting a church where there was a rather temperamental loudspeaker system in operation. Being warned about it, he tapped it experimentally before he began the service. It didn't seem to be operating and so he muttered, 'There's something wrong with this thing.'
The congregation, hearing only a murmur, thought he had begun the service and had said, 'The Lord be with you.' So they dutifully replied, 'And also with you.'

☺☺☺☺☺

According to the 'Anglican Digest', the Bishop of Blackburn telephoned a church dedicated to the Holy Trinity, and heard the vicar answer crisply, 'Holy Trinity.' To this the Bishop replied, 'How nice to get through without saying one's prayers!'

(Church Times - Portugal Street Diary)

☺☺☺☺☺

During the Pope's visit to Canterbury, his followers begged Dr Runcie to have a word with the Holy Father to insist that he should take a rest, for the Pope would not listen to them.
The Archbishop agreed and took the Pope to one side. Smiling, the Pope agreed, saying: 'When in Canterbury, you do as Canterbury does.'

(re-told from report in Sunday Express)

The Rt. Rev. David Sheppard, during his Dimbleby Lecture in 1984, told of a man who introduced his (the Bishop's) wife as, 'This is Mrs Bishop, the wife of the famous footballer.'

☺ ☺ ☺ ☺ ☺

The Rt. Rev. R Williamson, in his enthronement sermon as Bishop of Bradford, chose the text, 'Here I am among you like a servant.' He promised that he would not spend all his time on a pedestal, and added, 'People who come down from pedestals can be a blessed nuisance.' *(Church Times)*

☺ ☺ ☺ ☺ ☺

The sermon our preacher rt. rev.
Preached may have been a rt. clev.,
    But his theme, though consistent,
    Kept the end so far distant,
That we left, for we thought he mt. nev.

(Church Times - Portugal Street Diary)

☺ ☺ ☺ ☺ ☺

A clerical comment on a kindly Dean: If the Dean found himself in Hell, he would look round and would say, 'What a lot of interesting people - and how thoughtful of them to have lit a fire!'

☺ ☺ ☺ ☺ ☺

Advice to young ordinands: 'You have to preach, whether you can or cannot; but if you don't strike oil in five minutes, then stop boring!'

☺ ☺ ☺ ☺ ☺

A very young cleric bounded up the pulpit steps, full of confidence. His sermon, however, was a disaster, and he came down the steps, bowed and humble. An old man said to him, 'If tha'd gone up as tha came down, tha'd have come down as tha went up.'

☺ ☺ ☺ ☺ ☺

A chaplain in the television studios says that as he wanders around the place, he is often asked, 'What are you in . . . ? - or are you real?'

(retold from 'Church Times')

☺ ☺ ☺ ☺ ☺

A minister who was about to move to another church went to say goodbye to one of the old ladies in the town. She insisted that the next incumbent would not be as good as he had been. Rather flattered, the minister asked why. The lady replied, 'I've been worshipping here for over fifty years, and each new minister has been worse than the last one.'

☺ ☺ ☺ ☺ ☺

A certain curate had difficulty with his sermons. The Bishop advised him to borrow one of his books and read from it. The curate did so, and began solemnly reading his sermon the following Sunday with the words, 'When I was Bishop of ......'.

☺ ☺ ☺ ☺ ☺

Vicar at PCC Meetings: 'Would anyone like the visiting missionary for lunch on Monday?'

☺ ☺ ☺ ☺ ☺

A vicar was asked to preach in a remote country church. He took a taxi and arrived to find that the congregation was made up of the verger and one other man.
'Hardly worth holding a service,' joked the vicar in a friendly voice.
'Oh but I would like to hear your sermon,' said the one man.
So the vicar went ahead with the service as planned. It was not until some time later that he found out that the one man had been the taxi driver whom he did not recognise without his hat. He was paid by the hour and was therefore hoping for a long service before taking the vicar back.

(re-told from 'Keep Smiling' - by C.W. George [Arthur H Stockwell])

☺ ☺ ☺ ☺ ☺

A clergyman was asked to preach at a church where long sermons were the usual thing. He prepared a long address, but found that, on delivery, it came out rather shorter than he had intended. He apologised to the congregation and explained that his dog had come into his study while he was preparing the talk and must have chewed up some of its pages.
After the service, the verger came up to the preacher, and said quietly, 'That is a very useful dog of yours. Do you think you could let our own vicar have one of its pups?' *(Ibid)*

☺ ☺ ☺ ☺ ☺

A cleric in a hurry parked his car and put a note on the windscreen which read, 'Have been round this square ten times; am in a hurry for an appointment. Forgive us our trespasses.'
When he returned there was a parking ticket for him together with another note, which read, 'Have been round the square ten years. If I don't book you I shall lose my job. Lead us not into temptation.'

☺ ☺ ☺ ☺ ☺

The restaurant waiter eyed the vicar askance as he began to say a silent grace before beginning his meal.
'There's no need to say your prayers, sir,' he said huffily. 'We have a very good chef here.' *(from 'The Beacon', Barrow-in-Furness)*

The vicar arrived home after a hard day in the parish. His wife said to him, 'I apologise for talking shop, dear, but you really do look as miserable as sin.' *(Ibid)*

☺ ☺ ☺ ☺ ☺

Too late, the vicar remembered he had forgotten to invite one of the old ladies of the parish to the vicarage garden party. She had never missed in previous years. In haste, the vicar sent the curate to get her.

She refused to come, saying, 'It's too late to ask me now, young man, I've already prayed for rain.' *(re-told from Old Hove Record)*

☺ ☺ ☺ ☺ ☺

The vicar had been in hospital for some time. During his absence the Church Council met and decided they should send him a Get Well message. It read, 'Church Council met today and wished you a speedy recovery by 11 votes to 10.'

☺ ☺ ☺ ☺ ☺

c) EPITAPHS
On the tombstone of a lawyer named Strange were the words:
"Here lies an honest lawyer, that's Strange.'
(from 'Keep Smiling' by C.W. George [Arthur H Stockwell])

☺ ☺ ☺ ☺ ☺

The local council was discussing the building of a wall round the cemetery, but one rustic councillor thought the project was quite unnecessary.

'Where's the need of it?' he asked. 'Those that are in can't get out, and those that are out don't want to get in.'

☺ ☺ ☺ ☺ ☺

Unintentional Humour on a Gravestone in India:
'Sacred to the memory of Rev. .... who, after twenty years of unremitting labour as a missionary, was accidentally shot by his native bearer.
Well done, thou good and faithful servant.'

☺ ☺ ☺ ☺ ☺

The next two are **Epitaphs seen in Yorkshire churchyards,** *quoted by Nicholas Rhea in 'Constable on the Prowl' publ. by Robert Hale.*
Here I lie, no wonder I'm dead,
The wheel of a wagon went over my head.

☺ ☺ ☺ ☺ ☺

Sudden and unexpected was the end
Of our esteemed and beloved friend.
He gave to his friends a sudden shock
By falling into Sunderland Dock.

Epitaph from Eastwell, Kent:
Fear God,
Keep the Commandments, and
Don't attempt to climb a tree,
For that's what caused the death of me.
(from 'I wish I'd said that' by Nick Harris [Octopus])

☺ ☺ ☺ ☺ ☺

Epitaph on a 17th Cent. Locksmith:
A zealous locksmith died of late,
And did arrive at Heaven's gate.
He stood without and would not knock,
Because he meant to pick the lock. *(Ibid)*

d) FROM PARISH MAGAZINES AND OTHER LITERATURE

From an Irish Parish Bulletin:
'There will be a procession next Sunday afternoon in the grounds of the monastery: but if it rains in the afternoon, the procession will take place in the morning.'

☺ ☺ ☺ ☺ ☺

From a Parish Bulletin in the USA:
'In medieval times churches were not heated. Please add one dollar to your weekly pledge to make sure this custom is not revived.'

☺ ☺ ☺ ☺ ☺

Sign outside a Church in Nottingham:
Come inside and have your faith lifted.

☺ ☺ ☺ ☺ ☺

Two signs *seen in the rear window of a car in Leeds:*
   'Put your trust in the Lord.' –
   and underneath it:
   'This car is protected by Krooklok'.   *('The Beacon', Barrow-in-Furness)*

☺ ☺ ☺ ☺ ☺

Notice in a Church Hall:
'Will the ladies responsible for making tea, kindly empty tea-pots and kettles and then stand upside down in the sink.'

☺ ☺ ☺ ☺ ☺

From a Cheshire Church Magazine: quoting a newspaper report:
'The sudden fierce gust of wind took all who were at the ceremony completely by surprise. Hats were blown off and copies of the vicar's speech and other rubbish were scattered over the site.'

A Notice in a Berkshire Church read:
'Photographs of the church and the vicar (interior and exterior) may be had from the verger.'

☺ ☺ ☺ ☺ ☺

A report in a Welsh paper stated that 'There was a good number present at the Bible class on Monday and a keen discussion took place on the subject, "Are there stages of sin?" Later in the evening a practical class was held.'

☺ ☺ ☺ ☺ ☺

Misprint: 'Evensnog' is at 6pm this week.

☺ ☺ ☺ ☺ ☺

A lady at a church service suddenly realised she had forgotten her collection, so she put her watch on the plate as a token gesture. The next hymn included the lines, 'Lord, her watch Thy Church is keeping...'

☺ ☺ ☺ ☺ ☺

WRONG CUE
A jeweller's assistant, an absentminded fellow, was being married. He was presenting the bride with the ring when he hesitated.
"With this ring," prompted the minister.
"With this ring," said the bridegroom," we give a written guarantee, reminding the customer that the price will be refunded if it is not as represented."

☺ ☺ ☺ ☺ ☺

NOT SO CLEAR
A noted minister preaching one Sunday was asked by the soprano soloist for his subject so that she might select an appropriate solo to follow the sermon. When he hesitated, she said, 'Never mind. I'll listen carefully and before you are through. I'll have something appropriate ready.'
The sermon ended. Then came the selection entitled, 'Sometime, Somewhere, We'll Understand.'

☺ ☺ ☺ ☺ ☺

An advertisement in a For Sale Gazette:
"Record-breaking 1920's gramophone"

☺ ☺ ☺ ☺ ☺

AUTHOR'S ACKNOWLEDGEMENTS

Every effort has been made to trace any copyright holders and to seek their permission for items in this book. However, it is not at all easy to trace the origin of an anecdote or joke. Stories are passed on, told and re-told, so that it becomes almost impossible to find the original source. Some of the items in this book have been heard in sermons or talks; others have been seen in parish magazines or newsletters, often without any source being given. Where sources are known, they are acknowledged in the text or listed here.

In the case of items seen in books or periodicals, written permission has been sought, and such is noted here.

(1) Written permissions have been received from:- Church Times; Church Teacher (later 'Together'); London Weekend Television; Arthur H Stockwell (from the book 'Keep Smiling'); R.S.C.M. (items in 'The Cassock Pocket Book' and 'Church Music'); Sunday Express; and Octopus Books ('I wish I'd said that' by Nick Harris).

(2) For items which have been told by word of mouth, sometimes by more than one person, the author is indebted to: Prof R Moss, Mr C James, Mrs C Earle, Mrs M Philippe, Canon T A Rockley, Mrs J Harrop, Mrs F Marrow, Mrs E Hudson, Mrs J Pollard, Rt Rev R Williamson, Canon B T Young, Rev G Brown, Mrs M R Marr (in 'Share'), Mrs J Abbott, Mr and Mrs R Hunt, Mrs M Dawson, Mrs A Flinn, Mrs A Dodgson, Miss K Colbeck, Mrs M Sadler.

(3) Verbal permission was given by the leader of the Children's Council in 1965 in Hereford, for some thirty-three items, mainly one-liners which appeared in 'The Child Learns'.

(4) For items for which written permission has not been sought, because the items were very short or were re-told: 'Bits & Pieces' Ripon; 'The Beacon' Barrow-in-Furness; Lancashire Magazine; Scripture Union; 'St Stephen-by-Saltash' Parish News; 'Share' (Chester Diocese); 'Wife to the Archbishop' by Anne Arnott (The life story of Jean Coggan - published by Mowbrays); 'Constable on the Prowl' by Nicholas Rhea - published by Robert Hale; and Old Hove Record.

(5) Finally to Miss J E Bellamy, who typed the script.

MOORLEY'S

We are growing publishers, adding several new titles to our list each year. We also undertake private publications and commissioned works.

Our range of publications includes:

Books of Verse:
Devotional Poetry
Recitations
Drama
Bible Plays
Sketches
Nativity Plays
Passiontide Plays
Easter Plays
Demonstrations
Resource Books
Assembly Material
Songs and Musicals
Children's Addresses
Prayers and Graces
Daily Readings
Books for Speakers
Activity Books
Quizzes
Puzzles
Painting Books
Church Stationery
Notice Books
Cradle Rolls
Hymn Board Numbers

Please send a stamped addressed envelope (approx. 9" x 6") for the current catalogue or consult your local Christian Bookshop who should stock or be able to order our titles.